UNLOCKING THE SECRETS OF PROPERTY INVESTMENTS

LAMLA JULY

DEDICATION

This book is dedicated to those who are willing to learn about Real Estate on how to purchase property in many different ways and want to build the economy in 2023

INTRODUCTION

In the ever-evolving world of real estate, property management plays a crucial role in ensuring the smooth operation and profitability of properties. Whether you are a seasoned investor or a novice looking to enter the real estate market, understanding the intricacies of property management is essential for success. This comprehensive guide written by Lamla July, a 19-year-old aspiring author, aims to provide readers with a comprehensive understanding of property management principles and practices.

Lamla has written a comprehensive book on property management, providing readers with valuable insights, strategies, and practical advice for navigating the real estate industry. The book covers various aspects of property management, including leasing, maintenance, tenant relations, financial management, and legal considerations. Whether you are an experienced property manager looking to improve your skills or a beginner entering the field, this book aims to equip you with the knowledge and tools needed to succeed in real estate. Lamla draws on years of industry experience to create a comprehensive resource that covers every aspect of property management. The book covers topics such as property marketing, leasing, maintenance, financial management, tenant relations, legal considerations, and special considerations for different types of properties.

"Unlocking the Secrets of Property Management: The Complete Guide to Real Estate" is a valuable resource for property managers looking to excel in their profession.

TABLE OF CONTENT

COVER

TITLE PAGE

COPYRIGHT

DEDICATION

INTRODUCTION

CHAPTER ONE
THE FUNDAMENTALS OF REAL ESTATE

CHAPTER TWO
TYPES OF REAL ESTATE INVESTMENT

CHAPTER SIX
PROPERTY MANAGEMENT

CHAPTER SEVEN
LEGAL CONSIDERATIONS IN REAL ESTATE

CHAPTER EIGHT
REAL ESTATE DEVELOPMENT

CHAPTER NINE
USING DEBT TO GET RICH

CHAPTER ONE

THE FUNDAMENTALS OF REAL ESTATE

Definition of Real Estate

Real estate is a term for property that includes land, structures, and natural resources like crops, minerals, or water.It includes not only the actual structures but also the legal rights connected to possessing or making use of the property. Real estate is a significant asset class that is essential to many facets of society, including investment, trade, and housing.

Different forms of Real Estate

Residential properties are those made with living space in mind. They can be single-family homes or multi-unit structures like apartments or condominiums. Vacation homes and second homes used for recreational purposes can also be considered to be residential real estate.

For business purposes, commercial properties are used. They can be workplaces, shops, hotels, dining establishments, and shopping malls. For their operations, businesses typically lease or rent commercial real estate.

For manufacturing, production, or storage needs, industrial properties are used.
Factories, storage facilities, distribution hubs, and research facilities can all be included.
Real estate for industrial use is frequently found in areas or zones that have been designated as such. Agricultural activities are conducted on properties used for agriculture. They can be farms, ranches, orchards, vineyards, or farms with livestock. Farming and animal husbandry are the main uses of agricultural real estate. Every type of real estate has its own distinct qualities and factors to take into account. Location, size, amenities, and market demand are typically taken into account when determining a residential property's value. Commercial properties are frequently valued based on their potential for income and the success of the businesses housed there. The value of industrial properties may depend on elements like their proximity to transportation infrastructure or the presence of specialized facilities. Agri-properties may be valued based on elements like crop yield potential, water accessibility, and soil quality.

The real estate sector has a sizable impact on both the economy and society at large. Housing is provided for individuals and families, business operations and economic development are facilitated by commercial properties, manufacturing and production are supported by industrial properties, and food production is aided by agricultural properties.

PROPERTY RIGHTS

Property rights refer to the legal framework that controls who owns, uses, and transfers property. They are an essential component of contemporary societies and are essential for fostering social harmony, personal freedom, and economic growth. Although the legal framework governing property ownership differs between jurisdictions, it typically consists of laws, rules, and court judgments that specify and safeguard the duties and rights of property owners

OWNERSHIP RIGHTS INCLUDE :

The right to own property is one of the most important aspects of property rights. Exclusive control over a specific piece of property, such as land, buildings, vehicles, intellectual property, or other tangible or intangible assets, is granted to individuals or entities through ownership. Owners have the freedom to use, possess, enjoy, and dispose of their property however they see fit, as long as they stay within the bounds of the law.

A PACKAGE OF RIGHTS

Property rights frequently refer to a **"bundle of rights"** because they include a variety of entitlements that property owners have. Typical examples of these rights are:

1. Owners have the right to physically occupy their property and to prevent unauthorized users from using it.

2.Owners have the freedom to use their property however they see fit, provided that they do not interfere with the rights of others or break any laws or regulations that may be in force.

3.Owners have the freedom to give their property away, sell it, lease it, or give it as a gift.

4. Owners have the right to prevent unauthorized individuals from using or entering their property.

5. Owners have the right to take pleasure in the advantages and fruits of their property.

6. Owners have the legal right to decide how their property is used and maintained.

These rights are not unrestricted and may be subject to limitations due to zoning laws, environmental regulations, issues with public health and safety, governmental use of eminent domain, and contractual obligations.

OWNERS' OBLIGATIONS INCLUDE THE FOLLOWING

Property ownership comes with obligations in addition to rights. Owners are expected to uphold their duties to make sure that their property does not violate the rights of or cause harm to third parties. Property owners frequently have the following obligations:.

1. Maintenance and Care: Owners are in charge of keeping their property safe and livable and making sure it complies with all relevant building codes and safety regulations.

2. Owners are responsible for paying all property taxes as well as any other fees or assessments levied by the government or other relevant authorities.

3. Compliance with Laws and Regulations: Owners are responsible for adhering to any and all applicable laws, rules, and restrictions that pertain to their property, including zoning laws, environmental laws, and building codes.

4. Owners may be held responsible for damages caused by their property if it puts others at risk or causes harm to them.
Legal repercussions, such as fines, penalties, or even the loss of ownership rights, may follow failure to meet these obligations.

Legal Protection of Property Rights:

Laws safeguard property rights to ensure that owners can exercise them freely and without unjustified interference. Common legal defense measures include:.

1.Registration of property titles is required by many jurisdictions in order to create accurate ownership records and avoid disagreements.

2. Deeds and Contracts: Deeds or contracts are frequently used to formalize property transactions. These documents set forth the terms of transfer and offer ownership proof.

3. Legal Remedy: In the event that a property owner's rights are violated, the owner may file a lawsuit and request legal remedies like eviction orders, damages, or injunctions.

Additionally, intangible assets like patents, copyrights, trademarks, and trade secrets are safeguarded by intellectual property rights (IPR). These privileges give sole authority over the use and financial exploitation of inventive works.
In the legal framework governing property ownership, property rights play a crucial role. They impose certain obligations while also giving people and organizations the legal groundwork to possess, use, transfer, and enjoy their property.

Forging economic growth, attracting investment, and upholding social order all depend on the protection of property rights.

MARKET ANALYSIS

Understanding the real estate industry requires a strong grasp of market analysis. It entails investigating a range of market-influencing variables, such as supply and demand dynamics, economic indicators, and demographic trends. Market participants can get a better understanding of the state of the market and make wise decisions about buying, selling, or investing in real estate by looking at these factors.

Dynamics in supply and demand are one of the main factors affecting the real estate market. Property prices and rental rates are greatly influenced by the balance between the number of available properties (supply) and the number of prospective buyers or tenants (demand).

Prices generally go down when supply outpaces demand, while they go up when the imbalance is the other way around.

In order to spot trends and foresee future market conditions, market analysis involves monitoring changes in supply and demand.

Understanding real estate markets also heavily relies on economic indicators. The growth of the GDP, employment rates, inflation, interest rates, and consumer confidence are just a few variables that can have a big impact on the demand for real estate

For instance, there is frequently a rise in housing demand during times of economic expansion marked by low unemployment rates and rising incomes. In contrast, demand may fall during economic downturns or recessions as people become more wary of making significant financial commitments.

The analysis of the real estate market must also consider demographic trends. The demand for various types of properties can be greatly impacted by changes in population size, age distribution, household formation rates, and migration patterns. For instance, an aging population may result in greater demand for retirement communities or assisted living facilities. Similar to the previous example, an influx of young professionals into a specific area may increase demand for starter homes or rental apartments.

Numerous data sources and analytical tools are used to conduct a thorough market analysis. These comprise:

1. Real estate market reports: Numerous organizations regularly release reports that offer in-depth analyses of particular real estate markets at the local, regional, and/or national levels. These reports frequently include information on real estate prices, sales volume, rental rates, vacancy rates, and other important market indicators. Reports from renowned real estate companies like CBRE, JLL, and Colliers International are some examples of reliable real estate market analyses.

2. Government Data: A wealth of data that can be used for market analysis is gathered and published by government organizations at the local, state, and federal levels. This includes data on housing starts, building permits, employment trends, demographics of the population, and economic indicators. Among the well-known sources of government information is the U.S.Federal Reserve, Census Bureau, and Bureau of Labor Statistics.

3.Associations in the field: Through their publications and research reports, real estate industry associations frequently offer insightful analyses of the market. These organizations have access to information and knowledge specific to the real estate industry and represent various sectors of the sector. The National Association of Realtors (NAR), Urban Land Institute (ULI), and National Multifamily Housing Council (NMHC) are a few examples of reputable industry associations.

Understanding real estate markets requires a thorough process called market analysis. Market participants can learn a great deal about the state of the market and make wise decisions by looking at variables like supply and demand dynamics, economic indicators, and demographic trends. Among the most reliable sources used in conducting in-depth market analyses are real estate market reports, government data sources, and trade associations.

CHAPTER TWO

TYPES OF REAL ESTATE INVESTMENT

Residential Properties : Properties classified as residential are those whose primary purpose is to serve as homes or lodging for individuals or families. These buildings are built with the intention of giving residents a secure and comfortable place to live.
Single-family homes, apartments, condominiums, townhouses, and mobile homes are just a few examples of residential properties. Different lifestyles and preferences are catered for by the unique characteristics and features of each type of residential property.

Single-family residences are unattached buildings that are typically occupied by one family. They provide exclusivity and a sense of ownership because the home and land are owned by the homeowner only. Single-family homes come in all shapes and sizes, from tiny cottages to enormous mansions.
On the other hand, apartments are multi-unit structures where each unit is rented out to a different tenant. Apartments offer shared amenities like parking spots, laundry facilities, and recreation areas and are frequently found in urban areas. They give people and families who might not be able to afford a single-family home a more affordable housing option.

Condominiums, also referred to as condos, are similar to apartments in that they contain multiple units in one structure. Condominiums, in contrast to apartments, in which units are rented, are privately owned by residents. While having exclusive ownership over their individual units, condo owners share ownership of the building's common areas, including the hallways, elevators, and recreational facilities.

In addition to single-family homes and condominiums, townhouses are another type of residential property. Townhouses frequently have several levels and are made up of a number of paired units. There may be shared walls between units, but each one has its own entrance. Townhouses provide a good balance between solitude and communal living.

Last but not least, **mobile homes**—also referred to as manufactured homes or trailers—are prefabricated buildings that can be moved to different locations. When residents lease the land on which their homes are built, they live in designated communities or parks where mobile homes are common. These homes offer flexibility for those who prefer a more transient lifestyle and are an affordable housing option.

Residential properties serve as more than just physical structures; they are also settings for personal and family memories, social connections, and sense of home. They offer safety, comfort, and a place for one's own expression. There are various ownership options available in addition to the various kinds of residential properties.

Homeownership, in which individuals or families buy a property and have full ownership rights,
 is the most typical type of residential property ownership. Another choice is to rent, whereby people or families shell out money each month to live in a house that belongs to someone else.

Commercial Property : Office buildings, retail establishments, industrial facilities, and hotels are examples of real estate properties that fall under the category of commercial properties. These properties are typically owned by people, companies, or real estate investment trusts (REITs) and are leased or rented to businesses for various commercial activities. Due to the fact that they give businesses a place to call home and support the creation of jobs and a thriving economy, commercial properties are essential to the economy. For a variety of industries, including finance, retail, manufacturing, hospitality, and others, they act as the physical infrastructure.
Office buildings are among the most prevalent kinds of commercial real estate. These are buildings that have been created especially to house office-based businesses. Office buildings can be small single-tenant structures or big skyscrapers with many floors and tenants. They frequently come with amenities like common areas, parking lots, and conference rooms. Among commercial real estate, retail spaces are another important type.

These include malls, strip malls, one-store operations, and other places where merchants deal directly with customers to sell goods or services. Storefronts, display windows, and signage are examples of features that may be present in retail spaces, which are frequently built in high-traffic areas to draw customers. Industrial facilities are commercial buildings that are used for production, warehousing, distribution, or R&D operations. Depending on the particular industry they serve, these properties can have a wide range of sizes and layouts. Loading docks, powerful equipment, and storage spaces are common features of industrial facilities.Businesses that cater to travelers by offering temporary lodging and related services are known as hotels and hospitality properties. These can range in size from modest bed and breakfasts to sizable luxury resorts. Guest rooms, restaurants, meeting spaces, fitness centers, and swimming pools are common hotel amenities.For eople or organizations looking to generate long-term income or experience capital growth, investing in commercial properties can be a tempting option. The potential benefits of investing in commercial real estate include stable rental income, tax advantages, portfolio diversification, and potential property value growth over time.There are a number of things to consider before investing in commercial real estate. These factors include location, market demand, property condition, tenant quality, lease terms, and potential risks. Making informed investment decisions requires thorough due diligence and collaboration with knowledgeable professionals like real estate agents, attorneys, and property managers.

To ensure the efficient operation and financial viability of the assets, managing commercial properties entails a variety of duties. Tasks like acquiring and keeping tenants, negotiating leases, collecting rent, maintaining and repairing the property, managing finances, and adhering to local laws are the responsibility of the property owners or the property managers they have chosen.

Various trends and developments have had an impact on the commercial real estate market recently. Among them are the growth of coworking spaces, which offer adaptable office solutions for freelancers and small businesses; the impact of e-commerce on retail spaces; sustainability initiatives driving green building practices; and technological advancements enhancing property management procedures.

It should be noted that commercial properties are crucial elements of the business environment. They give different industries places to operate and help the economy grow. A long-term source of income and potential appreciation can be found in commercial real estate investments. Careful attention must be paid to tenant relations, maintenance, finances, and compliance when managing these properties. For businesses to adjust to shifting market dynamics, staying informed about industry trends is essential.

BENEFITS AND RISKS OF INVESTING IN OFFICE BUILDINGS

Commercial properties refer to real estate properties that are used for business purposes, such as office buildings, retail spaces, industrial facilities, and hotels. These properties are typically owned by individuals, corporations, or real estate investment trusts (REITs) and are leased or rented out to businesses for various commercial activities.

Commercial properties play a crucial role in the economy, as they provide spaces for businesses to operate and contribute to job creation and economic growth. They serve as the physical infrastructure for a wide range of industries, including finance, retail, manufacturing, hospitality, and more.

One of the most common types of commercial properties is office buildings. These are structures specifically designed to accommodate office-based businesses. Office buildings can range from small single-tenant buildings to large skyscrapers with multiple floors and tenants. They often include amenities such as conference rooms, parking facilities, and common areas.

Retail spaces are another significant category of commercial properties. These include shopping malls, strip malls, standalone stores, and other spaces where retailers sell goods or services directly to consumers. Retail spaces are typically located in high-traffic areas to attract customers and may include features like storefronts, display windows, and signage.

Industrial facilities are commercial properties used for manufacturing, warehousing, distribution, or research and development activities. These properties can vary widely in size and layout depending on the specific industry they serve. Industrial facilities often have specialized infrastructure such as loading docks, heavy-duty machinery, and storage areas.

Hotels and hospitality properties are commercial establishments that provide temporary accommodation and related services to travelers. These can range from small bed-and-breakfast establishments to large luxury resorts. Hotels often feature amenities like guest rooms, restaurants, conference facilities, fitness centers, and swimming pools.

Investing in commercial properties can be an attractive option for individuals or entities looking for long-term income generation or capital appreciation. Commercial real estate investments offer potential benefits such as steady rental income, tax advantages, portfolio diversification, and potential appreciation in property value over time.

When considering investing in commercial properties, several factors should be taken into account. These include location, market demand, property condition, tenant quality, lease terms, and potential risks. Conducting thorough due diligence and working with experienced professionals such as real estate agents, lawyers, and property managers is crucial to making informed investment decisions.

Managing commercial properties involves various responsibilities to ensure the smooth operation and profitability of the assets. Property owners or their appointed property managers are responsible for tasks such as tenant acquisition and retention, lease negotiations, rent collection, property maintenance and repairs, financial management, and compliance with local regulations.

In recent years, the commercial real estate industry has been influenced by various trends and developments. These include the rise of coworking spaces, which provide flexible office solutions for freelancers and small businesses; the growth of e-commerce impacting retail spaces; sustainability initiatives driving green building practices; and technological advancements enhancing property management processes.

Commercial properties are essential components of the business landscape. They provide spaces for various industries to operate and contribute to economic growth. Investing in commercial properties can offer long-term income generation and potential appreciation. Managing these properties requires careful requires careful attention to tenant relationships, maintenance, financials, and compliance. Staying informed about industry trends is crucial for adapting to changing market dynamics.

Industrial Properties: Properties that are specifically built and used for industries are referred to as industrial properties. These real estate holdings could consist of factories, warehouses, distribution centers, logistics hubs, and other comparable buildings. Investors, developers, and occupiers must be aware of the distinctive features of industrial real estate in order to make wise choices and realize the full potential of these assets.The practical design of industrial properties is one of their distinguishing characteristics. Industrial properties are primarily focused on offering effective spaces for production, storage, and distribution activities, in contrast to other types of commercial real estate, such as office buildings or retail locations. Due to the need to accommodate heavy machinery and equipment, industrial buildings frequently have high ceilings, spacious floor plans, wide column spacing, and specialized infrastructure. Specifically constructed for the production of goods, manufacturing facilities are a type of industrial property. These facilities can be small businesses or huge factories with numerous production lines. They frequently have areas designated for assembly lines, storage facilities for unfinished goods and finished goods, loading docks for shipping and receiving, and occasionally even offices for administrative tasks.
By acting as hubs for the storing and distributing of goods, distribution centers play a crucial part in the supply chain.

For the most effective movement of goods, these facilities are placed in close proximity to transportation networks like highways, railroads, or ports. With automated storage and retrieval systems (AS/RS) or high-density racking systems, distribution centers frequently have extensive storage capabilities. To facilitate the seamless transfer of goods between various modes of transportation, they also include loading docks, truck courts, and occasionally cross-docking areas.

Similar to distribution centers in terms of size, logistics hubs act as regional or national distribution points. To maximize the flow of goods across various regions, these hubs are strategically positioned at important transportation intersections. Logistics hubs may provide value-added services like packaging, labeling, sorting, or product customization in addition to storage and distribution options. They frequently have cutting-edge technology systems for order fulfillment, inventory management, and shipment tracking.

Industrial properties stand out from other types of real estate due to a number of distinctive qualities. Specialized utilities and infrastructure are one example of such a characteristic. Depending on the type of industrial activities being conducted, industrial buildings may need particular electrical supply capacities, water and wastewater treatment systems, ventilation and exhaust systems, or even specialized environmental controls.

The cost and viability of developing or retrofitting industrial properties can be significantly impacted by these infrastructure needs.

The location of industrial properties is another crucial feature. The success of industrial operations depends on the proximity to labor markets, transportation networks, suppliers, and consumers. Access to major roads, railroads, airports, or ports can lower transportation costs and increase the effectiveness of the supply chain. For industries that require specialized workforce, the proximity of skilled labor is another important factor. The development of industrial properties may also be influenced or restricted by local zoning laws and the land that is available there.

Numerous factors, such as the state of the economy, business trends, technological developments, and consumer behavior, have an impact on the demand for industrial properties. For instance, as e-commerce has grown, there is a greater need for logistics and distribution centers to support online retail operations. Similar technological developments in the manufacturing sector, such as automation and robotics, have increased the demand for modern manufacturing facilities with adaptable floor plans and sophisticated infrastructure.

The term "industrial properties" refers to a broad category of real estate holdings that are created and used specifically for industrial purposes. Investors, developers, and occupiers who want to make wise choices about these properties must be aware of their distinctive features.

Industrial real estate has a distinctive character that is influenced by its practical design, specialized infrastructure needs, strategic location considerations, and changing market dynamics

SPECIALIZED INDUSTRIES : The term "specialized properties" refers to real estate holdings that serve particular industries or sectors, such as healthcare facilities, educational institutions, recreational properties, and mixed-use developments. These niche markets have particular needs and expect specialized amenities.

1. Healthcare Facilities:
Hospitals, clinics, medical office buildings, and assisted living facilities are just a few examples of the diverse types of properties that make up healthcare facilities. These buildings are made to offer patients medical services and care.Modern medical technology, specialized treatment spaces, patient rooms with cutting-edge monitoring systems, and simple accessibility for patients with disabilities are just a few examples of specialized features in healthcare facilities.In this industry, it's essential to follow zoning laws and healthcare regulations.

2.Institutions of higher learning:
Schools, colleges, universities, and research facilities are examples of specialized real estate in the education sector.These characteristics are created to make learning and research activities easier.

Institutions of higher learning need dormitories, sports facilities, administrative offices, laboratories, and libraries.
While adhering to accessibility guidelines and safety regulations, the design of these buildings should encourage a positive learning environment.

3.Recreational Buildings:
Recreational properties are used for entertainment and leisure activities..
Theme parks, hotels, golf courses, sports facilities, and social clubs are a few examples.
These properties frequently have features like swimming pools, fitness centers, dining establishments, theaters, and outdoor recreation areas. Recreational properties are designed to give visitors pleasurable experiences while ensuring safety precautions are in place.

4. Mixed-Use Developments:

Multiple property types are combined in a single project or complex under the heading of mixed-use developments. They typically mix residential, commercial, retail, and entertainment spaces. The goal of mixed-use developments is to build thriving neighborhoods where people can live, work, and play close to one another. Such features as pedestrian-friendly designs, green areas, and communal amenities (e.g), fitness centers, or rooftop gardens), as well as a variety of retail choices.

Investigating niche markets like healthcare facilities, educational institutions, recreational properties, and mixed-use developments necessitates a thorough understanding of the particular requirements and regulations related to each industry. In-depth market research is required for real estate developers and investors interested in these specialized properties, including examinations of supply, demand, rivalry, and potential profitability.

CHAPTER THREE

FINANCING REAL ESTATE INVESTMENTS

Mortgage Basics

A mortgage is a contract that a borrower and a lender enter into that enables the borrower to get money to buy a property, usually real estate. It is a kind of loan where the asset being bought or refinanced serves as security. The property is pledged as collateral for the loan by the borrower (also known as the mortgagor), and the lender (also known as the mortgagee) has the right to seize the property if the borrower does not repay the loan in accordance with the terms set forth in the mortgage. The mortgage agreement outlines a number of terms and conditions, including the loan amount, interest rate, repayment plan, and any other clauses that were reached an understanding on by both parties. The Borrower shall make timely principal and interest payments, usually on a monthly basis, towards the Loan. While interest is the cost of borrowing money, principal is the initial sum that was borrowed. To finance the purchase of residential or commercial properties, both individuals and businesses frequently use mortgages. They give borrowers access to sizable amounts of cash that they might not otherwise have. Lenders get paid for lending their money by adding interest to the loan balance.

Various types of mortgages are available depending on a number of variables, including the interest rate structure, the repayment terms, and the eligibility requirements. Typical types include:.

1.**Mortgage with a fixed interest rate:** The interest rate for this type of mortgage remains the same over the course of the loan. By maintaining a constant monthly payment over time, it offers borrowers stability and predictability.

2.The interest rate on an adjustable-rate mortgage (ARM) may change over time depending on the state of the market. Usually, it begins with a fixed rate for a short time (e.g., 5 years), after which it periodically adjusts based on a predetermined index.

3.Mortgages that are backed by the government, such as those that are insured by the Federal Housing Administration (FHA), the Department of Veterans Affairs (VA), or the U.S.USDA, the department of agriculture. Compared to conventional mortgages, they frequently offer lower down payment options and eligibility requirements that are more lenient.
By making property ownership and investment easier, mortgages have a big impact on the real estate market. They enable people and companies to buy properties that they might not be able to afford upfront by spreading the cost over a long time. By giving lenders a source of income and boosting the construction and

housing-related industries, mortgages also help the economy as a whole.

A mortgage is a contract that allows borrowers to get money to buy or refinance real estate. It entails using the asset as collateral for the loan and making interest-only payments over a predetermined time frame. Mortgages come in a variety of forms, including fixed-rate, adjustable-rate, and government-insured choices, to accommodate various borrower needs and preferences

Alternative Financing

Alternative financing is any unconventional way to raise money for a variety of goals, including starting or growing a business, funding a project, or buying assets. It presents substitutes for the traditional borrowing from banks and seeking venture capitalist investment. This in-depth response will cover a variety of alternative financing methods, such as crowdsourcing, peer-to-peer lending, angel investing, and more.

Crowdfunding is one well-liked type of alternative financing. Crowdfunding entails collecting modest sums of money from a large number of people, typically via online platforms. Crowdfunding comes in a variety of forms, including debt crowdfunding, equity crowdfunding, and crowdfunding based on rewards.

Donation-based crowdfunding is when people give money to a cause or project without hoping to get anything in return. The funding of artistic endeavors like movies or music albums using this type of crowdfunding is quite common.

People can donate money to reward-based crowdfunding campaigns in exchange for non-monetary rewards or tangible goods. For instance, a business might reward campaign contributors with early access to a product or special merchandise. Through equity crowdfunding, people can make investments in businesses in exchange for equity or shares. This type of crowdfunding has grown in popularity because it enables smaller investors to take part in early-stage investments that were previously only available to venture capitalists or angel investors.

Peer-to-peer lending or crowdlending, also referred to as debt crowdfunding, is the practice of people lending money to organizations or people in need. The loan process is facilitated by online platforms that link borrowers and lenders. The platform and the borrower's creditworthiness both affect interest rates and repayment terms.

Peer-to-peer lending (P2P lending) is another alternative financing method. P2P lending platforms match up individual lenders who are eager to lend money to borrowers at competitive interest rates. In order to evaluate borrowers' creditworthiness and determine interest rates, these platforms frequently use algorithms and credit scoring models.

Another option for alternative financing is angel investing. High-net-worth individuals known as angel investors lend money to start-ups or early-stage businesses in exchange for equity ownership. They frequently offer the businesses they invest in not only financial resources but also knowledge and connections to the industry.With venture capital (VC), experienced investors fund start-ups or small businesses with significant room for expansion. Compared to angel investors, venture capitalists typically make larger investments and frequently participate actively in the management and strategic choices of the businesses they back.Thanks to technological advancements, alternative financing has grown beyond what was previously possible. For instance, the development of Initial Coin Offerings (ICOs) as a type of alternative financing has been made possible by blockchain technology. By offering investors digital tokens or cryptocurrencies in exchange for fiat money or other recognized cryptocurrencies, ICOs enable businesses to raise capital.Alternative financing choices have also become available, especially for small businesses and entrepreneurs. These include revenue-based financing, where companies receive money in exchange for a portion of their future earnings, and merchant cash advances, where companies get cash up front in exchange for a percentage of their future sales.

Alternative financing offers a variety of options for people and businesses looking for funding outside of traditional banking channels. It provides adaptability, accessibility, and the possibility of cutting-edge funding solutions. Prior to making any decisions, it is crucial to carefully weigh the risks and advantages of each alternative financing option.

Risk Management: Risk management is an important consideration in financial planning and decision-making for individuals, companies, and organizations. It entails locating potential risks, evaluating their potential effects, and putting strategies in place to reduce or mitigate those risks. Several strategies, such as insurance coverage, contingency planning, and diversification, can be used in the context of financial risks.

One of the most important methods for minimizing financial risks is insurance coverage. Insurance protects against potential losses by assigning the risk to an insurance provider in exchange for recurrent premium payments. To cover different types of risks, different insurance policy types are available. For instance, people can buy health insurance to cover medical costs, life insurance to support their dependents financially in the event of their demise, and property insurance to protect their assets from theft or damage.

Companies choose various insurance coverage options in the business world depending on their unique requirements. Typical types of business insurance include property insurance (covering tangible assets like buildings and equipment), liability insurance (defending against lawsuits), and business interruption insurance (reimbursing lost revenue as a result of unforeseeable events). Individuals and companies can transfer the financial risk connected to specific events or circumstances to the insurer by putting in place the necessary insurance coverage.An additional vital technique for controlling financial risks is contingency planning. In order to address potential risks or unforeseen events, contingency planning entails creating alternate strategies or backup plans. This proactive approach lessens the negative financial effects of unfavorable circumstances.

When it comes to individuals, contingency planning may entail setting up an emergency fund to pay for unanticipated costs like unexpected medical expenses or lost income. People can create a financial cushion that they can draw upon in times of need by regularly setting aside a portion of their income.Similar to this, businesses should have backup plans in place to deal with potential risks. This might entail creating contingency budgets to deal with unforeseen costs, creating disaster recovery plans to ensure business continuity in the event of natural disasters or technological failures, and having backup suppliers in case the primary supplier is unable to deliver goods or services.Spreading investments across various assets or asset classes is referred to as diversification, and it is a risk management strategy. Individuals and businesses can lessen the effect that a single investment's poor performance will have on their overall financial well-being by diversifying their investment portfolios.

By investing in a variety of different asset classes, including stocks, bonds, real estate, and commodities, one can achieve diversification in the context of personal finance. This lessens the risk brought on by a single investment performing poorly. For instance, if other investments perform well, the effect on the overall portfolio of one stock experiencing a significant decline in value will be lessened.Similar to how individuals can diversify their lives, businesses can do the same by entering new markets or sectors. This lessens their reliance on a single product or market, making them less susceptible to market downturns or risks unique to their industry. To build a more balanced and resilient organization, diversification can also involve adding new product lines or buying complementary businesses.

Reducing financial risks necessitates a thorough strategy that incorporates diversification, contingency planning, and insurance coverage. By shifting the risk to an insurer, insurance protects against potential losses. Creating backup plans for unanticipated risks or events is known as contingency planning. To mitigate the effects of subpar performance in any one area, diversification spreads investments across various assets or markets. Individuals and companies can manage financial risks and protect their financial wellbeing by using these strategies.

CHAPTER FOUR

REAL ESTATE VALUATION

Appraisal Methods

The process of calculating a property's value is called real estate appraisal.The value of real estate assets is estimated by appraisers using a variety of techniques. The sales comparison approach, the income capitalization method, and the cost approach are some of these techniques.One of the most widely used techniques in real estate appraisal is the sales comparison approach, also referred to as the market approach or market data approach. This strategy compares the subject property to comparable properties that have recently sold nearby. To ascertain the property's fair market value, the appraiser considers elements like its location, size, condition, and amenities. When there are enough comparable sales available, this method is especially helpful.The income capitalization method is mainly employed to value properties that generate income, such as rental apartments, office buildings, or retail establishments. Using a property's potential for income, this method determines an estimate of its value.To determine the present value of upcoming cash flows produced by the property, the appraiser factors in things like rental income, operating costs, vacancy rates, and market capitalization rates. This approach is predicated on the idea that investors will offer a specific price for a piece of real estate based on its potential to generate income.The cost approach, also referred to as the replacement cost method, works by figuring out how much it would cost to replace a given piece of property with one that has similar value.

When there aren't enough comparable sales or income data available, this method is frequently used to assess special-purpose properties like schools, churches, or government buildings. In order to arrive at an estimated value, the appraiser calculates the cost of constructing a property similar to it at the going rate and subtracts any depreciation or obsolescence.Other methods may be employed in addition to these three fundamental appraisal techniques, depending on the particulars of the property being valued. These include the gross rent multiplier method and the residual land value method, which determines the value of vacant land based on its potential for development.It is crucial to remember that the appraisal process necessitates a blend of objective data analysis and subjective judgment. Both quantitative and qualitative factors, including the condition of the property and its location, must be taken into account by appraisers. The complete analysis of the property's value should be included in the final appraisal report, along with a description of the techniques used and any underlying assumptions.

There are many different techniques used in real estate appraisal to determine a property's value. The income capitalization method makes value estimates based on potential income, while the sales comparison approach compares the subject property to recently sold comparable properties. The cost approach determines replacement cost. Depending on the particular situation, other strategies might also be employed. In their analysis, appraisers must take into account both objective data and subjective opinion

Market Analysis

Market analysis is an important step in the real estate investment process. This includes conducting thorough research to assess the various factors that can affect property values, rents, vacancy rates and potential return on investment. Market analysis helps investors make informed decisions and increase their chances of success in the real estate market.One of the most important aspects of market analysis is real estate valuation. This involves examining recent sales data for similar properties in the area to determine current market value. Factors such as location, size, condition and amenities can affect property value. Additionally, analyzing past trends and anticipating future changes in the local real estate market can provide valuable insight into potential increases or decreases in property values.

Another important issue in market analysis is recruitment. Investors should assess the demand for rental properties in a particular area and determine the appropriate rental rate to achieve. This includes researching comparable rental offers and considering factors such as location, property type, size, conditions and amenities.

Understanding the dynamics of the rental market can help investors assess potential rental income and assess the feasibility of an investment.

Vacancy plays an important role in assessing the profitability of real estate investments. High vacancy rates mean there is an oversupply of affordable housing, which can lead to increased competition and lower rents. Conversely, a low vacancy rate indicates strong demand for rental properties and likely high rental income. By analyzing historical vacancy rates and current market conditions, investors can assess the level of risk of a particular investment opportunity.

Market analysis also allows investors to estimate potential return on investment (ROI). This includes calculating key financial metrics such as cash flow, cap rate and return on equity. Cash flow analysis takes into account both rental income and expenses related to owning and managing the property. Breakeven rate is calculated by dividing net operating income by the value of assets and represents the profitability of assets. Return on equity measures the return on an investor's initial investment and helps evaluate the overall performance of an investment.

Investors can use a variety of information sources for comprehensive market analysis. These include real estate market reports, industry publications, government data, and online platforms that provide access to historical real estate sales data and. Additionally, networking with local real estate professionals such as real estate agents, appraisers and property managers can provide valuable insight into local market conditions.Market analysis is an important step in real estate investing. This includes conducting comprehensive research to estimate property values, rents, vacancy rates and potential return on investment. By analyzing market conditions and trends, investors can make informed decisions and increase their chances of success in the real estate market

Due Diligence

The evaluation of a property's state, legal standing, and likelihood of future appreciation is a critical process called due diligence. Before making any investment decisions, it entails conducting a thorough investigation and analysis to make sure that all pertinent information about the property is gathered and evaluated. These comprehensive steps, which are listed below, typically comprise several crucial steps.

1.**Inspection of the Property**: The inspection of the property is the first stage of due diligence. This entails physically inspecting the structure or surrounding area in order to evaluate its general state, structural soundness, and any potential problems or defects. For a thorough assessment of the property and a comprehensive report on its current condition, a professional inspector may be hired.

2. A **title search** is done to make sure the property is actually owned legally and to look for any liens or encumbrances that might make it more difficult to sell. To confirm that the seller has a clear and marketable title to the property, this procedure involves looking up public records like deeds, mortgages, and court documents. It also aids in locating any legal problems or claims that might affect the use or worth of the property in the future.

3. **Environmental Assessment**: To find out if the property poses any environmental risks, it is essential to conduct an environmental assessment. In order to determine the presence of hazardous materials, soil contamination, or other environmental concerns, this evaluation typically entails reviewing historical records, visiting the site, and running tests. For both assessing

potential liabilities and complying with the law, it is crucial to comprehend these risks.

4. **Zoning and Land Use Analysis**: In order to ascertain the property's present and potential future uses, it is critical to assess the zoning laws and land use restrictions that apply to it. This step involves checking the property's alignment with intended uses and any upcoming developments in the area by reviewing local zoning laws, comprehensive plans, and other applicable regulations.

5. **Market Analysis**: A thorough market analysis can be used to determine whether a property is likely to increase in value in the future. Aspects like supply and demand dynamics, recent sales information for comparable properties, rental rates, vacancy rates, and general market trends are all evaluated during this analysis. The potential for long-term appreciation of the property can be better understood by being aware of the market dynamics and forecasts.

6.**Financial Analysis**: To ascertain the property's profitability and potential return on investment, it is essential to evaluate its financial aspects. In order to assess the property's potential for cash flow and overall financial performance, this analysis also includes reviewing income and expense statements, lease agreements, rental histories, and other financial documents.

7. **Legal and Regulatory Compliance**: It is crucial to confirm that the property complies with all rules, laws, and permits that may be relevant. In order to ensure compliance with building codes, zoning laws, environmental laws, and any other pertinent requirements, this step entails reviewing permits, licenses, certificates of occupancy, and other legal documents.

8. **Professional Consultation**: During the due diligence process, consulting with experts like real estate lawyers, accountants, appraisers, or consultants can be very helpful. These professionals can offer advice on risk mitigation and assist in identifying potential risks or issues that might not be obvious to non-specialists.Investors can gain a complete understanding of a property's condition, legal status, and potential for future appreciation by conducting a thorough due diligence process that includes these crucial steps. Making informed investment decisions and reducing the risks involved in real estate transactions require the use of this information

Evaluation of Property condition

Assessment of a property's general condition and quality is a crucial step in the process of property condition evaluation. To ascertain the state of a property prior to buying or selling it, it is typically conducted by professionals like home inspectors, appraisers, or real estate agents. Both buyers and sellers can use this assessment to help them make wise choices and bargain for reasonable prices.

The term "property condition evaluation" refers to a variety of aspects of a property, such as its structural integrity, mechanical systems, electrical systems, plumbing, roofing, insulation, and general maintenance. The evaluation aims to find any current or potential issues that might call for maintenance or renovations. It also aids in calculating the market value of the asset and offers an estimate of the asset's remaining useful life.Professionals thoroughly examine both the interior and exterior of the property during a property condition evaluation. They look for signs of damage or deterioration in the foundation, walls, floors, ceilings, windows, doors, and other structural elements. Additionally, they evaluate the efficiency and security of the plumbing, heating, and cooling systems, as well as the appliances and fixtures.
A property condition evaluation may also include testing for environmental dangers like lead-based paint, asbestos, radon gas, mold, or pests in addition to visual inspections. For the occupants' health and safety to be guaranteed, these tests are crucial.A thorough report outlining the conclusions and suggestions is typically the end result of the evaluation process. Buyers can use this report as a useful tool to bargain with sellers over fixes or price drops. It assists sellers in anticipating potential problems so they can fix them prior to listing the property.

Evaluating Legal status & Potential for future appreciation

When assessing the legal standing and potential for future growth of a specific asset or investment, it is important to take into account a number of factors that may have an effect on its worth and expansion prospects.

The legal system in place to protect the asset, market demand and trends, prevailing economic conditions, the regulatory environment, and any potential risks or uncertainties are among these factors.

Legal Standing:

A resource's acceptance and recognition by the law are referred to as its legal status.

The specifics of this can change depending on the jurisdiction and the kind of asset that is being assessed. Real estate properties, for instance, are governed by property laws, whereas financial market authorities regulate stocks and securities.

To ensure adherence to relevant laws and regulations, it is essential to comprehend the legal context of the asset.

Possibility of Future Appreciation:

The likelihood that the value of an asset will rise over time is referred to as the asset's potential for future appreciation.Market demand, supply and demand dynamics, economic conditions, technological advancements, and regulatory changes are just a few of the variables that may have an impact on this potential. Assessing these elements can assist in determining whether an asset has the potential for long-term growth and appreciation.

Market trends and demand:

The potential for an asset to increase in value depends heavily on market demand.
Future demand levels can be predicted by understanding market trends and consumer preferences.
Real estate, for instance, may be affected by variables like population expansion, urbanization, infrastructure improvement, and shifting demographics.
The same is true for financial markets, where knowledge of market dynamics and investor sentiment can be used to predict whether stocks, bonds, or other financial instruments will increase in value.

The state of the economy is.

The value of assets is directly influenced by the state of the economy.The performance of an asset can be affected by variables like the GDP growth rate, inflation rates, interest rates, employment rates, and consumer confidence.Because a strong economy encourages more consumer spending and investment activity, it usually creates favorable conditions for asset appreciation.

Environmental Regulation:

The legal standing and potential for asset appreciation are significantly influenced by the regulatory environment.
Both positive and negative effects on asset values can result from regulatory changes.
For instance, favorable regulations that encourage investment or offer tax breaks can boost demand and propel appreciation.On the other hand, tighter rules or adjustments to tax laws may depress market sentiment and have an effect on an asset's value.

Risks and Uncertainties:

When determining a financial asset's potential for future growth, it is critical to evaluate the risks and uncertainties attached to that asset.The value of an asset can be affected by a variety of variables, including market volatility, geopolitical risks, legal disputes, environmental concerns, technological disruptions, and competitive forces.One way to find potential obstacles and uncertainties that might affect the asset's growth prospects is to conduct a thorough risk analysis. Assessing the legal standing and potential for future appreciation of an asset necessitates a thorough examination of a number of variables, including the legal framework, market demand and trends, economic conditions, regulatory environment, and risk factors. Investors can determine the likelihood of their investments growing by taking these factors into account.

CHAPTER FIVE

REAL ESTATE INVESTMENT STRATEGIES

1.Buy and Hold

A buy-and-hold strategy is a long-term investment strategy that involves the purchase of real estate with the aim of generating rental income and potentially benefiting from price appreciation over time. This strategy is commonly used by real estate investors looking to build wealth through passive income and long-term capital growth.

The basic premise of a buy-and-hold strategy is to buy assets with the intention of holding them for an extended period of time, often years or even decades. The investor's goal is to generate regular rental income from the tenants while also benefiting from the potential to increase the value of the property over time. By holding ownership for the long term, investors can capitalize on market cycles and leverage the power of compounding returns. One of the main advantages of a buy and hold strategy is its ability to generate passive income. Rental properties can deliver consistent cash flow, which can be especially attractive to investors looking for regular income or looking to supplement existing income. Rental income can help cover mortgage payments, property maintenance costs, and other costs associated with owning real estate.
A buy-and-hold strategy allows investors to benefit from the potential for an asset's value to increase over time. Real estate has historically shown bullish trends over the long term, although it's important to note that there are no guarantees. By holding assets for an

extended period of time, investors increase their chances of catching any potential market upside.

Another benefit of a buy-and-hold strategy is the potential for tax benefits. Rental properties offer various tax deductions, including mortgage interest, property taxes, insurance premiums, repair costs, and depreciation. These deductions can help reduce taxable rental income and potentially reduce overall tax liability for investors.

However, it is important to consider some of the potential challenges associated with a buy-and-hold strategy. Property management can be demanding, requiring landlords to manage tenant issues, property maintenance, repairs, and other responsibilities. In addition, the real estate market can experience fluctuations, which can affect property values and rental demand. Investors should carefully analyze market conditions and select properties in locations with strong rental demand and upside potential.

To effectively implement a buy-and-hold strategy, investors should conduct thorough research and thorough due diligence before purchasing a property. This includes analyzing market trends, assessing rental demand, assessing the condition of the property, and estimating potential rental income and costs. It is essential to consider factors such as location, property type, neighborhood amenities, proximity to schools and transportation, and general market conditions.

In addition, investors should also consider long-term financial goals and risk tolerance when implementing a buy-and-hold strategy. Real estate investing requires capital, and building a diversified portfolio of rental properties can take time. Investors should assess their financial situation, investment horizon, and ability to handle potential vacancies or unexpected expenses. Buy-and-hold strategy is a long-term investment approach that involves buying real estate for rental income and upside potential. This strategy allows investors to generate passive income, benefit from the potential increase in the value of the property, and possibly benefit from tax advantages. However, it requires careful research, wealth management skills and a long-term vision to succeed.

2.FIX AND FLIP

A real estate investment strategy known as "fix and flip" entails buying properties in need of repair, putting them through renovations, and then reselling them for a profit. To ensure a successful outcome, this process necessitates careful planning, investigation, and execution. We will go over every step of the fix and flip process in detail in this thorough explanation.

1.How to Spot a Property in Distress.

Finding distressed properties with the potential for profitable renovations is the first step in the fix and flip process. Properties classified as distressed are typically those that are in bad shape, have been abandoned or neglected, or are in danger of going into foreclosure. Finding foreclosed homes is possible in a number of ways:

Online listings: Real estate portals and marketplaces frequently feature listings for distressed properties. These listings might include foreclosed homes, short sales, or houses that require extensive repairs.

b) Networking: Establishing connections withwholesalers, real estate brokers& other business professionals can open doors to off-market distressed properties.

Finding potential deals can also benefit from networking with regional investors and from attending real estate events.

c) Direct Marketing: Some investors use direct marketing techniques like sending letters or postcards to homeowners facing foreclosure or focusing on particular neighborhoods known for their distressed property inventory.

Carrying out due diligence

Before making an offer on a potential distressed property, careful due diligence is necessary. This also comprises:

a) Property Inspection: It's essential to hire a qualified home inspector to evaluate the property's state. The inspection report will point out any structural problems, required fixes, or undiscovered issues that could have an impact on the renovation budget.

b) Title Search: By conducting a title search, you can make sure that the property is free and clear of any liens or other legal issues that might make the purchase process more difficult.

c) Market analysis: To ascertain the potential value of the property following renovation, it is essential to examine the regional real estate market. Studying recent comparable sales (comps), recent market trends, and local demand for renovated properties are all part of this process.

d) Renovation Budget: To determine the costs involved in bringing the property up to market standards, a thorough renovation budget must be created. Costs for supplies, labor, licenses, and any unanticipated expenses are included.

Paying for the Purchase

The next step is to secure financing after performing due diligence and determining that the property is a wise investment. For fix and flip projects, there are several financing options available:

a) Investors with good credit and a solid financial history may be eligible for a traditional mortgage loan. Contrary to other financing options, this one might have more stringent requirements and drawn-out approval procedures.

b) **Hard Money Loan:** Hard money lenders specialize in offering short-term loans specifically for real estate investments. Despite having higher interest rates and fees, these loans are typically easier to qualify for.

c) **Private Money Lenders**: Funding for fix-and-flip projects may come from private individuals or businesses. In comparison to hard money lenders or conventional banks, these lenders might provide more flexible terms.

d) **Self-Financing**: A few investors decide to pay cash for foreclosed homes. The requirement for financing is removed with this option, but the number of projects an investor can work on at once may be constrained.

4. **Renovation Procedure**:

The process of renovating the property starts after it is purchased. This includes :

a) **Creating a Renovation Plan**: A thorough renovation plan outlines all the repairs and enhancements required to bring the property up to market standards. This entails figuring out which areas of the property need repair, choosing the right materials, and estimating the cost.

b) **Hiring Contractors**: Employing contractors or subcontractors may be necessary, depending on the size of the project. Before choosing a contractor, it is essential to investigate them, check their references, and get several quotes.

c) **Obtaining Permits**: Depending on local laws, some renovations may need permits from the appropriate authorities. To prevent potential legal problems, it is crucial to make sure all required permits are obtained before work is started.

d) **Managing the Renovation**: To guarantee that the work is finished on schedule, within budget, and in accordance with the renovation plan, it is essential to supervise the renovation process. A successful renovation requires frequent site visits, open communication with the contractors, and prompt resolution of any problems.

5.The property will be advertised and sold.The last step in the fix and flip procedure is to market and sell the property after the renovation is finished. In order to maximize sales and draw in potential customers, effective marketing strategies are essential

Staging: Setting up a welcoming environment for potential buyers while staging the property can help it show off its potential. This entails setting up the furniture, adding accents, and maintaining the property's cleanliness and presentation.

b) **Professional Photography**: High-quality photographs of the renovated property can significantly enhance its online listing and marketing materials. Hiring professional photographer can capture the property's best features and attract more potential buyers.

c) **Listing the Property**: Utilizing online real estate platforms, social media, and local marketing channels can help reach a wide audience of potential buyers. Working with a real estate agent experienced in selling renovated properties can also be beneficial.

d) **Negotiating Offers**: Once offers start coming in, negotiating with potential buyers is essential to secure the best possible sale price. Evaluating each offer's terms, contingencies, and financing options is crucial in making an informed decision.

e) **Closing the Sale**: After accepting an offer, completing all necessary paperwork, inspections, appraisals, and meeting any other contingencies are required before closing the sale. Working with a real estate attorney or title company can ensure a smooth closing process.Fix&flip is a real estate investment strategy that involves purchasing distressed properties, renovating them, and selling them for a profit. The process includes identifying distressed properties, conducting due diligence, securing financing, managing renovations, and marketing/selling the property.

WHOLESALING

Wholesaling is a real estate investment strategy that involves finding properties off the market and selling deals to other investors for a fee. This practice allows wholesalers to profit from the difference between the contract price and the price at which they assign the contract.The wholesale process usually begins with the wholesaler identifying potential off-market properties. These properties often deteriorate or need repair, making them less attractive to traditional buyers. Wholesalers can use a variety of methods to find these properties, including networking with a real estate agent, participating in foreclosure auctions, searching public records, or using an online platform. dedicated route connecting wholesalers with motivated sellers. Once a potential property is identified, the wholesaler negotiates a contract of sale with the seller. The contract includes an assignment clause, which allows the wholesaler to assign his or her rights and obligations under the contract to another buyer. This clause is important because it allows the wholesaler to assign the contract without buying the goods himself. After securing the sale and purchase agreement, the wholesaler begins to market the property to other investors. They may use a variety of channels such as online advertising, social media platforms or their network of real estate investors. The goal is to find a buyer willing to take over the contract and close the property.
When a buyer is found, the wholesaler gives him a contract with a fee. These fees are often referred to as transfer fees and are negotiated between the wholesaler and the buyer. Fee amounts can vary depending on factors such as the value of the property, market conditions, and the wholesaler's negotiating skills.

It is important to note that wholesale is legal in most jurisdictions; however, there are some rules and restrictions that wholesalers should be aware of. For example, some states require wholesalers to have a real estate license or work under the direction of a licensed real estate broker. In addition, there may be specific disclosure requirements or limits on how much profit a wholesaler can earn from a transaction.Wholesaling can be an attractive strategy for real estate investors looking to generate income without significant capital or credit. By finding properties off the market and awarding contracts, wholesalers can earn fees while avoiding the costs and risks associated with buying and renovating the property. However, wholesale also has its challenges. Finding motivated sellers and getting a favorable purchase deal can be time-consuming and competitive. In addition, building a network of trusted buyers is crucial to successful wholesale, as finding a buyer quickly is key to closing a deal.Wholesaling is a real estate investment strategy that involves finding properties off the market and selling deals to other investors for a fee. It allows wholesalers to profit from the difference between the contract price and the price at which they assign the contract. While this can be a profitable strategy, wholesalers must comply with legal regulations and overcome various challenges to succeed in this field.

REAL ESTATE INVESTMENT TRUSTS (REITs)

Real estate investment trusts (REITs) are publicly traded companies that own and manage income-generating real estate portfolios. Investing in REITs can offer a number of benefits to investors, including diversification, liquidity, potential for long-term capital gains, and steady income distribution.One of the main benefits of investing in REITs is diversification. By investing in REITs, investors gain exposure to a diverse portfolio of real estate assets across sectors as diverse as residential, commercial, industrial, healthcare and hospitality. This diversification helps reduce risk by spreading investments across different assets and locations. In addition, REITs often have professional management teams with expertise in the acquisition, development and management of real estate. This allows investors to benefit from the knowledge and experience of these professionals.Another benefit of investing in REITs is liquidity. Unlike direct investments in real estate, which can be illiquid and require a lot of time and effort to buy or sell assets, REITs are traded on major exchanges. This means that investors can easily buy or sell REIT shares at market prices, giving them liquidity and flexibility. REITs also offer the potential for long-term capital appreciation. As the value of the underlying real estate held by the REIT increases over time, the value of the REIT's stock may also increase in value. This can lead to capital gains for investors as they sell their shares for a higher price than they originally paid.
Investing in REITs can ensure a stable income distribution. REITs are required by law to distribute at least 90% of their taxable income to shareholders as dividends. This means that investors can receive a steady stream of income from their investment in REITs.

REIT's dividend payout can be especially attractive to income-oriented investors looking for steady cash flow. It is important to note that investing in REITs also carries certain risks. The performance of REITs is influenced by many factors, including general property market conditions, interest rates, and economic trends. In addition, the value of REIT shares can fluctuate depending on investor sentiment and market conditions. Investors should carefully consider their investment objectives, risk tolerance, and conduct thorough research before investing in REITs.Investing in real estate investment trusts (REITs) can offer a number of advantages to investors. These include diversification, liquidity, potential for long-term capital gains, and regular income distribution. However, it is essential that investors evaluate their own financial goals and risk tolerance before making any investment decisions.

CHAPTER SIX

PROPERTY MANAGEMENT

Tenant Screening

Tenant screening is an important process for landlords and property managers to ensure they choose reliable tenants who will pay rent on time, take care of the property and respect it. terms of the tenancy agreement. Implement tenant screening best practices including conducting thorough background checks, checking references, and drafting comprehensive tenancy agreements. This comprehensive guide will outline the key steps and considerations involved in choosing a tenant.

1. **Screening process:**

Before starting the tenant selection process, it is important to establish clear criteria for selecting tenants. This may include factors such as income requirements, credit score thresholds, rental history, and criminal background checks. Clearly defining these criteria will help simplify the selection process and ensure consistency in the decision-making process.

2. **Registration process**:

The first step in the tenant screening process is to ask potential tenants to fill out a rental application form. This form will collect necessary information such as personal information, work history, income verification, previous address and references. It is important to obtain written consent from the applicant to perform a background check and verify the information provided.

3. **Background check**:

Background checks are an essential part of tenant screening. They help assess an applicant's creditworthiness, rental history, and criminal history. Here are the important things to consider when performing a background check.

a) **Credit check**:

Credit checks provide detailed information about an applicant's financial responsibility and payment history. This helps determine if they have a history of late payments or outstanding debt. Landlords can obtain credit reports from credit bureaus or use specialized tenant screening services to provide comprehensive credit information.

b) **Verify rental history**:

It is essential to contact the former owner or property manager to better understand the candidate's rental behavior. Questions may include whether they paid their rent on time, caused damage to the property, or breached the terms of the lease.

c) **Employment verification**:

Verification of an applicant's employment and income status helps assess their ability to pay rent. Requesting recent pay stubs or contacting their employer directly can help confirm their employment details.

d) **Judicial background check**:Criminal background checks are essential for the safety and security of the property and other tenants.

This verification can be done through local law enforcement agencies or specialized screening services.

4. **Check reference**:

In addition to checking hiring and employment history, you should contact the personal references provided by the applicant. These references can provide insight into a candidate's personality, reliability, and suitability as a tenant.

5. **Drafting the Tenancy Agreement**:

Once the right tenant has been selected, it is important to draft a comprehensive tenancy agreement that outlines the rights and responsibilities of both parties. The rental agreement should include details such as rent amount, payment due date, lease term, maintenance responsibilities, pet policy, and any additional rules or regulations specific to the property. .

6. **Legal compliance**:

During the tenant selection process, it is important to follow all applicable fair housing laws and regulations. Owners may not discriminate against applicants on the basis of protected characteristics such as race, color, religion, sex, national origin, marital status or disability. Familiarize yourself with the federal, state, and local laws governing tenant screening to ensure compliance.

Maintenance and Repairs

Maintenance and repair are essential aspects of property management. They involve ensuring that assets are properly maintained, taking preventive maintenance measures, and dealing with repair requests quickly and efficiently. This holistic approach maintains the value, function and aesthetics of the property while ensuring tenant or occupant satisfaction.

Property maintenance:

Property maintenance refers to the routine maintenance tasks required to keep the property in good condition. This includes interior and exterior maintenance activities. Interior maintenance can involve cleaning common areas, repairing or replacing appliances, servicing heating and cooling systems, inspecting and repairing plumbing and electrical systems, as well as deal with any other problems that may arise in the property.

Exterior maintenance focuses on maintaining the look and function of the property's external features. This includes landscaping, lawn maintenance, snow removal, gutter cleaning, roof inspection and repairs as needed. Regular testing is essential to identify potential problems early and prevent them from escalating into larger problems.

Preventive maintenance:

Preventive maintenance is a proactive approach to asset management that prevents equipment failure, minimizes downtime, and extends the life of various components of an asset. This involves performing regular checks, performing routine maintenance tasks, and following the manufacturer's recommendations.

Here are some common examples of preventive maintenance:

1. **Maintenance of HVAC system**:

Regular inspection and maintenance of heating, ventilation and air conditioning (HVAC) systems can help identify potential problems before they lead to system failure or reduced efficiency. Duties may include cleaning or replacing filters, lubricating moving parts, checking refrigerant levels, and ensuring proper airflow.

2. **Plumbing maintenance**:

Checking plumbing for leaks, blockages, or other problems can prevent water damage and ensure proper operation. This may involve checking for leaks in pipes or faucets, checking water heaters for signs of corrosion or faulty components, and regularly cleaning drains.

3. **Electrical system maintenance**:

Regular testing of electrical systems can help identify potential fire hazards or electrical problems. This may include checking for loose connections, checking circuit breakers and fuses, checking sockets and switches, and proper grounding. By implementing preventative maintenance measures, property managers can reduce the likelihood of unexpected breakdowns, minimize repair costs, and improve the overall safety and comfort of the propertenants

Handling repair requests:

Efficiently handling repair requests is critical to maintaining tenant satisfaction and resolving any issues that may arise in the property. Property managers need to establish clear communication channels for tenants to report repair needs quickly. This can be done through an online portal, email, phone call or a direct request.After receiving repair requests, the property manager must prioritize and categorize them based on urgency and severity. Emergency repairs that pose a safety or liveability risk should be handled immediately. Non-emergency repairs can be scheduled based on the availability of resources and contractors.Property managers must maintain a network of trusted, licensed contractors to handle different types of repairs. When selecting contractors, it's important to consider their expertise, reputation, pricing, and response times. Regular contractor performance reviews ensure that repairs are carried out to a high standard and in a timely manner. Additionally, property managers should keep detailed records of all repair requests, including the nature of the problem, the steps taken to fix the problem, and any costs involved. This document helps track trends in repair needs, identify recurring issues that may require more comprehensive solutions, and bring transparency to tenants

Rental Property Marketing

For rental properties to attract potential tenants and increase rental income, effective marketing strategies are essential. Landlords can make sure their vacancies are effectively advertised and appeal to the right target audience by putting into action a comprehensive marketing plan. Here are some important tactics to take into account:

1. **Online marketing**: In the current digital era, online marketing is one of the most efficient means of reaching a large audience of potential tenants. Landlords can reach a sizable pool of prospective tenants by advertising their vacant properties on well-known rental listing websites like Zillow, Trulia, Apartments.com, and Craigslist. These platforms enable landlords to post thorough property descriptions, top-notch images, and even virtual tours, all of which can significantly increase the rental property's visibility and appeal.

2.**Professional photography**: Attracting potential tenants depends heavily on the quality of the images. An important factor in attracting interest is hiring a professional photographer to take eye-catching photos of the property. Potential tenants may be persuaded to schedule viewings or request more information about the vacancy by viewing photos that are brightly lit and highlight the property's best attributes.

3. **Social media marketing**: Using sites like Facebook, Instagram, and Twitter to connect with potential tenants and reach a larger audience can be successful. You can share visually appealing content, such as pictures, videos, and property highlights, by setting up specific pages or accounts for your rental properties.

Building trust and drawing in more potential tenants can be achieved by engaging with followers by promptly responding to questions and sharing pertinent details about the neighborhood or nearby amenities.

4.**Referrals from current tenants**: One of the best ways to find dependable tenants is to ask them to recommend friends or family who may be looking for a rental property. Offering incentives to tenants, such as a referral bonus or reduced rent, can encourage them to tell their friends about the rental. Additionally, keeping good relations with current tenants by attending to their issues quickly and offering first-rate customer service can raise the possibility of getting recommendations.

5.**Advertising That Is Targeted**: For your rental property to be successfully marketed, you must comprehend the target market. Your chances of luring qualified tenants can be significantly increased by targeting the appropriate audience with your advertising campaigns. If you own a rental property close to a university, for instance, using college-specific platforms or bulletin boards to advertise can help you reach students who are actively looking for housing.

6. **Property Signage**: An age-old but still successful advertising tactic is to put a "For Rent" sign on the actual property. This strategy draws locals who might be considering relocating to the same neighborhood or region. Ensure that the signage is clear, visible, and includes contact information for inquiries.

7. **Virtual tours and 3D walkthroughs**: In recent years, the rental market has seen an increase in the popularity of virtual tours and 3D walkthroughs. These interactive tools allow potential tenants to explore the property remotely and get a realistic sense of its layout and features. Virtual tours can save time for both landlords and prospective tenants by narrowing down the list of properties to visit in person.

8. **Professional Property Descriptions**: Foremost in luring potential tenants is the creation of compelling property descriptions.

9. **Competitive Pricing**: Setting an appropriate rental price is vital for attracting tenants quickly while maximizing rental income. Conducting market research to understand the average rental rates in your area can help you determine a competitive price point. Pricing too high may result in extended vacancies, while pricing too low may lead to missed income opportunities. Consider factors such as location, property size, amenities, and market demand when determining the rental price.

10. **Prompt Communication and Follow-up**: Responding promptly to inquiries and scheduling property viewings efficiently is crucial for maintaining a positive impression with potential tenants. Make sure to provide multiple contact options, such as phone, email, or online forms, and respond to inquiries within 24 hours. Effective rental property marketing strategies involve a combination of online advertising, professional photography, social media marketing, word-of-mouth referrals, targeted advertising, property signage, virtual tours, compelling property descriptions, competitive pricing, and prompt communication.

By implementing these strategies, landlords can attract prospective tenants efficiently and maximize their rental income.
Highlighting unique features, amenities, and nearby attractions can make your rental property stand out from the competition.
Use descriptive language to paint a vivid picture of what it's like to live in the property and emphasize any recent renovations or upgrades.

CHAPTER SEVEN

LEGAL CONSIDERATIONS IN REAL ESTATE

Property law in South Africa covers a wide range of legal concepts governing title, contracts, zoning regulations, landlord-tenant law and environmental regulations. Familiarizing yourself with these important legal concepts is essential for anyone involved in the real estate industry in South Africa.

Ownership:

In South Africa, property rights are protected by the Constitution, which guarantees ownership of property. The Constitution also prohibits unfair discrimination on property rights. The Deed Registration Act of 1937 established the system of registration and transfer of property. This law ensures that all real estate transactions are recorded and provides legal certainty regarding property ownership.

Contract:

Contracts play an important role in real estate transactions in South Africa. The Land Transfer Act of 1981 regulates the sale and purchase of real estate. This law requires all land purchase agreements to be in writing and signed by both parties. It also defines specific requirements for the content of the contract of sale, including details of ownership, purchase price, and terms of sale. Partition rules:

Zoning regulations control how land is used and developed in South Africa. The Land Use and Planning Act 2013 (SPLUMA) is the primary law governing land use planning and zoning. SPLUMA establishes a framework for land use planning and land use management at the national, provincial and municipal levels. It empowers municipalities to develop zoning plans that govern land use within their jurisdiction.

Landlord-Tenant Law:

The landlord-tenant relationship is governed by the Rental Housing Act 1999. This law defines the rights and obligations of landlords and tenants with respect to residential rental property. It includes aspects such as rent increases, eviction proceedings, maintenance liability, and dispute resolution mechanisms. Lease Courts provide a forum for resolving disputes between landlords and tenants.

Environmental regulations:

Environmental regulations play an important role in the development and management of real estate in South Africa. The National Environmental Management Act of 1998 (NEMA) is the main legislation governing environmental protection. NEMA establishes a framework for environmental impact assessment, waste management, pollution control and natural resource conservation. It also defines the responsibilities of developers and landowners for compliance with environmental regulations.
Understanding key legal concepts such as title, contracts, zoning regulations, tenancy laws, and environmental regulations is crucial for anyone involved in the real estate industry. production in South Africa.

These laws provide a framework for conducting real estate transactions, protecting property rights and ensuring sustainable development

Taxation

Investors should be aware of the various tax implications associated with real estate investments in South Africa. These effects encompass 1031 exchanges, depreciation deductions, capital gains taxes, and property taxes. Investors must be aware of these tax implications in order to make wise choices and maximize their returns.

Property taxes.

The value of real estate that is owned by people or organizations is subject to property taxes. Rates and taxes are the term used in South Africa for property taxes. Local municipalities levy these taxes, which are then used to pay for services provided by the local government, including the construction, upkeep, and provision of services.
The municipal valuation of the property establishes the amount of property tax due. For the purpose of determining the market value of properties within a municipality, municipal valuations are periodically performed. The property's location, size, condition, and additions all play a role in its valuation.Depending on the rules established by the municipality, property owners must pay their property taxes annually or over a period of time. Penalties and legal ramifications may follow nonpayment of property taxes.

Taxes on capital gains.

When an investor sells real estate at a profit, capital gains tax (CGT) may be due.The Income Tax Act in South Africa regulates CGT.Based on the discrepancy between the property's selling price and its acquisition cost, the tax is calculated.In South Africa, a person's income tax bracket affects the CGT rate. Currently, the maximum CGT rate for individuals is 18%. But depending on the situation, some exclusions and deductions might be applicable. For instance, primary homes are typically exempt from CGT if certain requirements are met.The CGT rate is set at a fixed 22.4% for corporations and trusts. It's significant to remember that when selling South African real estate, non-residents may also be subject to CGT.

Deductions for depreciation:

Investors can recoup the cost of maintenance over time by taking depreciation deductions on their real estate investments. Depreciation deductions are claimed in South Africa under the wear and tear allowance system.Based on the cost of the asset, its anticipated useful life, and the investor's preferred method of depreciation, the wear and tear allowance is determined. South Africa recognizes the straight-line method and the diminishing balance method as two depreciation methods.In the straight-line method, a predetermined portion of the cost of the asset is subtracted annually over the course of the asset's anticipated useful life. The diminishing balance method enables an initial higher deduction that gradually decreases over time.It's important to remember that personal residences are not eligible for depreciation deductions; rather, they can only be used for properties that generate income.

The 1031 Exchanges.

1031 exchanges, which let investors postpone paying capital gains taxes by investing the proceeds from the sale of one property in another of a similar kind, are not specifically mentioned in South African law. However, Section 24B of the Income Tax Act contains comparable provisions.When a taxpayer sells an asset and reinvests the proceeds in another asset within a specific timeframe, Section 24B allows for a rollover relief. Individuals and businesses are both eligible for this relief. To ensure compliance with all pertinent laws and requirements, it's crucial to speak with a tax expert or lawyer.Investors should take into account the various tax implications of South African real estate investments. Local governments impose property taxes according to the property's value. Capital gains taxes are applicable when selling a property at a profit, with different rates depending on the taxpayer's status. To recoup the cost of wear and tear on properties that generate income, depreciation deductions can be made. While there is no specific provision for 1031 exchanges, Section 24B of the Income Tax Act offers options for similar rollover relief.

Risk Management

Risk management is an important aspect of land ownership in South Africa. Owners should resolve liability issues, review insurance options, and implement asset protection strategies to protect their investments. This holistic approach reduces potential risks and ensures the long-term viability of land ownership.

Liability issue:

Landowners in South Africa face many liability issues that need to be resolved. A significant concern is the potential for an accident or injury on the property. If a guest or tenant is injured by negligence or unsafe conditions, the landlord may be held liable. To reduce this risk, owners must ensure that their property complies with safety regulations and maintains a safe environment.Another liability issue concerns environmental risks. Owners should be aware of any potential environmental risks associated with their property, such as contamination or contamination. Failure to address these issues may result in legal liability and financial consequences. Conducting a thorough environmental assessment and taking appropriate corrective actions can help reduce these risks.

Insurance options:

Having adequate insurance is essential for homeowners in South Africa. There are a number of insurance policies available to protect against various risks associated with home ownership. Here are some popular coverage options:

1. **Property insurance**:

This type of insurance covers damage or loss to the physical structure of the property caused by perils such as fire, theft, vandalism or natural disaster. It usually includes coverage for buildings, fixtures, accessories, and sometimes even contents.

2. **Civil liability insurance**:

Liability insurance covers liability arising from third party injury or damage to the insured property. It protects homeowners from possible lawsuits and compensates for medical bills, legal fees, and other related expenses.

3. **Environmental liability insurance**:

This specialized insurance covers liability related to environmental risks and pollution incidents. It provides financial protection against legal claims, cleanup costs, and other costs associated with environmental damage. Choosing the right insurance options depends on the specific risks associated with the property and the owner's tolerance for risk. It is advisable to consult with insurance professionals who specialize in property insurance to determine the coverage that best suits individual circumstances.

Asset protection strategy:

Implementing asset protection strategies is crucial for property owners in South Africa to protect their investments. These strategies aim to protect assets from potential risks and legal claims. Here are some commonly used asset protection strategies:

1. Structure of land ownership

Asset owners can review their ownership structure through entities such as trusts, corporations, or partnerships. These structures can provide a layer of separation between personal property and real estate, reducing personal liability.

2. Limited Liability Company (LLC)

Forming an LLC can be an effective way to protect personal assets from potential liabilities related to ownership. By forming an LLC, the owner's personal liability is limited to the investment made in the business, thus protecting personal assets from legal claims against ownership. .

3. Main insurance contract:

In addition to standard coverage, owners may consider purchasing policies that provide additional liability protection beyond the limits of primary policies. These policies offer higher coverage limits and wider coverage, ensuring comprehensive asset protection. It is important for property owners to consult with legal and financial experts who specialize in asset protection strategies to determine the most appropriate method based on their particular situation and profile. their risk profile.

CHAPTER EIGHT

REAL ESTATE DEVELOPMENT

1.LAND ACQUISITION

Land acquisition is a complex process that includes identifying suitable development sites, negotiating sales contracts, and performing feasibility studies. This process is important for various stakeholders, including developers, investors and government organisations, as it lays the groundwork for future development projects. In this comprehensive answer, we will detail each step of the land acquisition process.

Determining suitable development sites:

The first step in land acquisition is to identify suitable development sites. This involves conducting extensive research and analysis to determine the potential of different sites. Factors to consider at this stage include the availability of infrastructure, proximity to amenities and transport networks, zoning regulations, environmental considerations, and market needs.To identify suitable development sites, developers often work with real estate agents, land brokers, or use geographic information system (GIS) technology. These tools help in analyzing different data sets such as population density, economic indicators, land use patterns, and demographic information. By considering these factors, developers can narrow their search to areas that match the purpose and goals of their project.

Negotiation of Purchase and Sale Contracts:

Once a suitable development site has been identified, the next step is to negotiate a purchase contract with the landowner. This involves entering into negotiations to determine the terms and conditions of the sale. The negotiation process usually includes discussions about pricing, payment terms, contingencies, and any other specific requirements or conditions.In this step, it is essential that both parties exercise accountability. Buyers should check the property's legal status, title, and any potential impediments or limitations that may affect its development potential. On the other hand, the seller can also conduct due diligence to ensure that the buyer has the financial ability to complete the transaction.To facilitate negotiations and ensure a fair deal for both parties, it is common for legal professionals such as a real estate attorney or a land acquisition specialist to participate. Their expertise helps in drafting legally binding contracts to protect the interests of all parties involved.

Carry out a feasibility study:

Once the sales contract has been negotiated and signed, the next step is to conduct a feasibility study. A feasibility study evaluates the viability and profitability of a development project on acquired land. These studies involve analyzing various factors such as market demand, financial projections, construction costs, legal requirements and potential risks.Feasibility studies are important because they provide developers with a comprehensive understanding of a project's potential return on investment (ROI) and potential challenges. They help determine whether the proposed development meets market needs and is financially viable.

If the feasibility study shows positive results, the promoters can proceed to apply for the necessary permits and financing for the project.

Land acquisition involves a multi-step process that includes determining a suitable development site, negotiating a purchase agreement, and conducting a feasibility study. Each step is critical to ensuring the success of land acquisition and subsequent development projects

PLANNING AND DESIGN

Planning and design procedures must take thoughtful design, architectural considerations, and sustainable development practices into account. These components are necessary for designing spaces that are useful, beautiful, and eco-friendly. This all-encompassing strategy guarantees that the built environment satisfies the requirements of its users while minimizing detrimental effects on the nearby ecosystem. We will discuss the significance of thoughtful design, architectural considerations, and sustainable development practices in this response.

Thoughtful Design:

A holistic approach to design that considers various aspects, including usability, aesthetics, user experience, and cultural context is considered to be thoughtful design. It strives to design areas that are not only aesthetically pleasing, but also effectively fulfill the functions for which they were intended. A thoughtful design takes the needs and preferences of the users into account to make sure the area is welcoming and improves their wellbeing.

Planning your space carefully is a crucial component of thoughtful design. This entails meticulously planning a space's layout to maximize its usability and flow. Designers can create spaces that are effective and simple to use by taking into account elements like traffic patterns, accessibility, and zoning laws.Aesthetics are a crucial factor in thoughtful design. Our experiences in a space are greatly influenced by aesthetics. A well-designed space considers factors like color schemes, lighting, materials, and textures to produce aesthetically pleasing environments that arouse positive feelings.Additionally, thoughtful design takes the cultural setting of a space into account. To ensure that the design is in keeping with its surroundings, it considers regional customs, values, and architectural styles. By using this strategy, you can preserve cultural heritage and foster a sense of place.

The following architectural considerations.

Architectural considerations cover a wide range of elements that affect the creation of designs. Structure, building codes and regulations, safety precautions, accessibility needs, and technological advancements are a few of these factors to take into account.One of the most important aspects of architectural considerations is structural integrity. Buildings must be constructed to withstand a variety of forces, including seismic activity, wind, and gravity. To make sure that the design is structurally sound and capable of withstanding these forces, structural engineers and architects collaborate closely.Architectural considerations also must take into account building codes and regulations. These codes establish requirements for energy efficiency, accessibility, fire safety, and building methods.

These guidelines must be followed by architects to guarantee that the structure complies with legal requirements and offers a secure environment for its occupants.Safety precautions are a key factor in the design of buildings. This entails creating environments that reduce risks and hazards, such as by including suitable lighting, signage, and emergency exits. To safeguard the users' health and welfare, architects must take potential risks into account when designing a structure.The design of buildings must also take accessibility into account. All people with different abilities should be able to use the space, and it should be inclusive. To ensure that everyone can comfortably navigate the space, it is necessary to include features like ramps, elevators, wide doorways, and tactile signage.Architectural considerations are also impacted by technological advancements. As technology develops so quickly, architects need to keep up with new building materials, methods, and sustainable building systems. Buildings that are more efficient and sustainable can result from incorporating these innovations into the design process.

Sustainable Development Practices:

To reduce the environmental impact of the built environment, sustainable development practices are crucial. By implementing these strategies, spaces that are socially just, environmentally conscious, and economically viable are created.Reducing energy consumption is one of the main objectives of sustainable development techniques. This can be accomplished using a variety of techniques, including implementing energy-efficient lighting systems, relying on renewable energy sources like solar panels or geothermal systems, and improving insulation to lower heating and cooling requirements.

Another important component of sustainable development practices is water conservation. To reduce water usage, designers can use efficient irrigation techniques, rainwater harvesting systems, and water-saving fixtures. Water within a building or site can also be treated and reused using wastewater treatment systems.Sustainable development practices give careful thought to material choice as well.Designers can select eco-friendly materials that are less harmful to human health, have a smaller carbon footprint, and are recyclable or biodegradable. Utilizing locally produced materials can lower emissions caused by transportation while also boosting regional economies.Sustainable development methods also place a strong emphasis on the need to protect ecosystems and natural resources.This can be accomplished by employing tactics like preserving green space, conserving biodiversity, and using permeable surfaces to lessen stormwater runoff and encourage groundwater recharge. Social equity and the well-being of the community are also given top priority in sustainable development practices. This entails designing spaces that are open to everyone, encouraging social interaction, and taking different user groups' needs into account. In order to ensure that the design reflects the aspirations and values of the local community, sustainable development practices frequently involve community engagement and collaboration.

PROJECT MANEGEMENT

In the construction sector, project management entails supervising and coordinating various aspects of a construction project, such as coordinating contractors, obtaining permits, managing budgets, and making sure the project is finished on time and within scope. The steps are listed below and are typically broken down into several steps:

1.Launch of the Project:

- Clearly define the project objectives. This is the first step in project management.
This entails figuring out the goal, the scope, and the deliverables.

- List all the parties with an interest in or who will be impacted by the project as stakeholders.
Clients, suppliers, workers, regulators, architects, engineers, and end users may all fall under this category.

- Perform feasibility studies: Evaluate the project's operational, legal, economic, and technical viability.
This assists in determining the project's viability and compatibility with the objectives of the organization.

2.Planning:

- Create a detailed project plan outlining the tasks, deadlines, resources needed, and dependencies for each stage of the building project. To visualize the project schedule, this entails creating a work breakdown structure (WBS) and a Gantt chart.

- **Distribute resources**: Establish the amount of labor, machinery, supplies, and subcontractors required for each task. To prevent delays, make sure that resources are accessible when required.Before beginning construction, identify all necessary permits and approvals from regulatory authorities and obtain them. This could include zoning permits, safety certifications, environmental clearances, and building permits.

- **Create a budget**: Determine the expenses related to each task and create an all-inclusive budget for the project. Throughout the course of the project, keep an eye on and manage costs to keep them within set limits.

3.**Execution**:

- **Coordinate contractors**: Pick and oversee contractors in charge of different facets of the construction project. This entails granting contracts, keeping tabs on how they're performing, resolving disputes, and ensuring that the project's requirements and quality standards are being met.

- Track construction project progress in accordance with the project plan on a regular basis. To address any problems or delays, this involves visiting the sites, going over the reports, and meeting with the stakeholders.

- **Handle changes**: Because construction projects are dynamic, changes may occur during the execution stage. Implementing suitable change management procedures and evaluating the effects of changes on the project's scope, schedule, and budget are essential.

- **Ensure quality and safety**: Put safety procedures into place to make sure that all workers engaged in the construction project are working in a safe environment. Monitoring and enforcing quality control procedures will also help to guarantee that the project complies with all requirements.

4. **Monitoring and management**:

- Monitor key performance indicators (KPIs) such as cost variance, schedule variance, quality metrics, and safety records continuously to track project performance. By doing so, deviations from the plan are easier to spot and corrective measures can be taken as needed.

- **Manage risks**: Identify potential risks that could have an impact on the project's success and create strategies to mitigate them. Maintain a continuous review and updating of the risk management plan.

- Interact with stakeholders: Keep lines of communication open with all parties concerned with the construction project. Provide frequent progress updates, address any issues, and control expectations.

5. **Project Completion:**

- **Carry out thorough final inspections**: Examine the finished construction project carefully to make sure it complies with all requirements and specifications.

- Obtain the necessary final approvals from clients and regulatory bodies before concluding the project.

- **Record key takeaways**: List the successes, difficulties, and best practices from the construction project. Future projects can be made better using this information.

- **Complete contracts**: Complete contracts with suppliers and contractors by making sure that all payments have been made and that any outstanding issues have been resolved.

- **Handover the project**: Return ownership of the finished building project to the client or end-user. Offering warranties, instruction manuals, and training could be part of this.Managing construction projects entails a number of steps, such as project initiation, planning, execution, monitoring and control, and project closure. Construction projects are guaranteed to be finished on schedule, within budget, and to the satisfaction of all parties involved with the project

CHAPTER NINE

DEBT TO PURCHASE PROPERTY

There are several different ways to use debt to buy property in the real estate market without having a credit score. Lenders typically prefer borrowers with good credit scores, but this isn't the only consideration they make when assessing loan applications. The following tips can assist you in navigating the procedure:.

1.**Create a Robust Financial Profile**: You can still show prospective lenders that you are financially responsible and stable even if you don't have a credit score. A stable income, a sizable savings account, and a low debt-to-income ratio are all good places to start when developing a sound financial profile. Based on these considerations, lenders will determine your capacity to repay the loan.

2. **Find Alternative Lenders**: Conventional banks and mortgage companies might be reluctant to give loans to people without credit scores. Alternative lenders, on the other hand, are experts at working with borrowers who have little to no credit history. When assessing loan applications, these lenders frequently take into account additional elements like income, employment history, and assets.

3.**Search for Seller Financing**: The owner of the property can also serve as the lender in a seller financing transaction. In this scenario, the seller agrees to finance all or a portion of the purchase price, allowing you to avoid getting a traditional mortgage by making regular payments to them instead.

In some cases, seller financing is more flexible and exempt from credit checks.

4. **Collateralize Other Assets**: If you have valuable assets, such as stocks, bonds, or other properties, you can use them as security to obtain a loan for the purchase of real estate. Lenders might be more willing to grant credit even if you don't have a credit score if you pledge these assets as security.

5.**Establish Relationships with Local Banks**: When looking for financing without a credit score, it can be helpful to have relationships with nearby banks or credit unions. These institutions frequently place a high value on interpersonal interactions and might be more open to working with borrowers who have consistently shown a commitment to responsible financial behavior.

6. If you have a trusted relative or friend with a good credit history, they might be willing to co-sign the loan or serve as a guarantor. This implies that in the event of a default, they will be liable for loan repayment. Possessing a co-signer or guarantor can give lenders extra security and improve your chances of getting financing.

7.**Increase your down payment by saving more money**: This will help make up for your low credit score. You can lower the amount of debt necessary and possibly increase your chances of getting financing by setting aside a larger sum of money to use for the purchase.

8.**Show Your Rental History**: If you have a history of paying your rent on time, this can show that you have the ability to manage your finances.

Lenders can better evaluate your creditworthiness by seeing proof of your rental history, such as canceled rent checks or landlord recommendations.

9.Consider working with a mortgage broker:
Mortgage brokers have access to a variety of loan products and lenders, including those who specialize in helping borrowers without credit scores. They can assist you in finding the best lender and assist you with the application.

10.Increase Your Creditworthiness: While this may not be a quick fix, taking steps to raise your creditworthiness over time can increase your chances of getting financing in the future. This entails opening credit accounts, making timely payments, and maintaining a low credit utilization rate. Although using debt to buy property in the real estate market may be difficult if you don't have a credit score, there are other options. Some practical strategies to think about include constructing a solid financial profile, looking for alternative lenders, investigating seller financing, collateralizing other assets, and forming connections with neighborhood banks. You can also improve your chances of getting financing by getting co-signers or guarantors, saving up for a bigger down payment, showing proof of your rental history, working with a mortgage broker, and enhancing your creditworthiness.

CONCLUSION

In summary, Unlocking the Secrets of Real Estate Investing is a comprehensive and informative book that provides readers with valuable information and strategies for successful real estate investing. Throughout the book, the author delves into different aspects of real estate investing, including understanding the market, analyzing potential properties, financing options, and managing risk. One of the strengths of this book is its emphasis on research and analysis. The author emphasizes the importance of thorough market research to identify profitable investment opportunities. By providing readers with practical tips and techniques for conducting market analysis, such as researching local trends, assessing supply and demand dynamics, and looking at economic factors, the book provides investors with the knowledge to make informed decisions. Additionally, "Unlock the Secrets of Real Estate Investing" provides in-depth guidance on property analysis. The author explains how to assess a property's value and potential by considering factors such as location, condition, rental income potential, and future growth prospects. By providing step-by-step instructions and practical examples, readers gain a better understanding of how to evaluate properties effectively. The book also covers the different financing options available to real estate investors. From traditional mortgages to innovative financing methods like seller financing or partnerships, the author explores different ways to finance real estate investments. This comprehensive approach ensures that readers have a variety of strategies to choose from depending on their financial situation and investment goals.Additionally, "Unlocking Real Estate Investment Secrets" discusses risk management in real estate investing.

The author emphasizes the importance of proper diversification and due diligence when building a real estate portfolio. By discussing common risks associated with real estate investments, such as market volatility, tenant problems, or unexpected expenses, readers will be better prepared to minimize these risks. that risk and protect their investment. "Unlocking Real Estate Investment Secrets" is a valuable resource for both new and experienced investors looking to improve their knowledge of real estate investing. With practical advice, comprehensive coverage of key topics, and an emphasis on research and analysis, this book provides readers with the tools and information needed to succeed in the real estate market. movables. The world of real estate offers endless possibilities for those willing to delve into its intricacies. This comprehensive guide has provided a solid foundation for understanding the fundamentals of real estate, various investment strategies, legal considerations, property management techniques, and future trends. Armed with this knowledge, readers can confidently navigate the dynamic landscape of real estate and make informed decisions to achieve their financial goals.

GLOSSARY

Appraisal: The process of determining the value of a property, usually conducted by a licensed appraiser. Appraisals are often required by lenders to ensure that the property's value is sufficient to secure the loan.

Assessed Value: The value assigned to a property by a government entity for the purpose of calculating property taxes. Assessed values are typically based on market value but may be subject to certain limitations or adjustments.

Closing: The final step in a real estate transaction where ownership of the property is transferred from the seller to the buyer. This typically involves signing legal documents, paying closing costs, and recording the transaction with the appropriate government agency.

Commission: A fee paid to a real estate agent or broker for their services in facilitating a real estate transaction. The commission is usually a percentage of the sale price and is typically paid by the seller.

Condominium: A type of housing where individual units are owned by separate individuals, while common areas and amenities are shared. Condominiums are governed by a homeowners' association (HOA) and may have specific rules and regulations.

Deed: A legal document that transfers ownership of a property from one party to another. The deed includes a description of the property, identifies the grantor (seller) and grantee (buyer), and is signed and notarized.

Escrow: A neutral third party, often an escrow company or attorney, holds funds and documents related to a real estate transaction until all conditions are met. This ensures that both parties fulfill their obligations before the transaction is completed.

Foreclosure: The legal process by which a lender takes possession of a property due to the borrower's failure to make mortgage payments. Foreclosed properties are typically sold at auction or through a real estate agent.

Homeowners' Association (HOA): An organization that manages and enforces rules for properties within a specific community or development. HOAs collect fees from homeowners to maintain common areas and enforce community guidelines.

Interest Rate: The percentage of the loan amount charged by a lender for borrowing money. Interest rates can vary based on factors such as creditworthiness, loan term, and market conditions.

Listing: A property that is available for sale or rent. Listings typically include information such as the property's price, location, features, and contact details for the listing agent or broker.

Mortgage: A loan used to finance the purchase of a property. The borrower (mortgagor) pledges the property as collateral to the lender (mortgagee) and makes regular payments over a specified period until the loan is fully repaid.

Multiple Listing Service (MLS): A database used by real estate agents and brokers to share information about properties for sale. MLS listings provide detailed information about properties, including photos, descriptions, and pricing.

Title: The legal right to ownership of a property. A title search is conducted to ensure that there are no liens, claims, or other encumbrances that could affect ownership.

Zoning: The division of land into different zones or districts with specific regulations regarding land use, building codes, and density. Zoning laws help control development and maintain the character of different areas within a jurisdiction.

Buyer's Agent: A real estate agent who represents the interests of the buyer in a real estate transaction. The buyer's agent helps the buyer find suitable properties, negotiates on their behalf, and assists with the closing process.

Equity: The difference between the market value of a property and any outstanding mortgage or liens on it. Equity represents the owner's stake in the property and can increase over time as mortgage payments are made or if the property appreciates in value.

Listing Agent: A real estate agent who represents the seller in a real estate transaction. The listing agent helps market and advertise the property, negotiate offers, and coordinate with other parties involved in the sale.

Lease: A legal agreement between a landlord (lessor) and a tenant (lessee) that grants the tenant the right to occupy a property for a specified period in exchange for rent.

Capitalization Rate: A measure used in real estate investment to determine the potential return on an investment property. It is calculated by dividing the net operating income by the purchase price or value of the property.

Easement: A legal right granted to someone to use another person's property for a specific purpose, such as accessing a neighboring property or utility lines.

Fair Housing Act: A federal law that prohibits discrimination in housing based on race, color, religion, sex, national origin, disability, or familial status.

Pre-approval: The process of obtaining a lender's commitment to provide a mortgage loan, based on an evaluation of the borrower's creditworthiness and financial situation. Pre-approval strengthens a buyer's position when making an offer on a property.

Title Insurance: Insurance that protects against financial loss due to defects in the title or ownership of a property. It provides coverage for legal expenses and potential claims against the property.

ABOUT THE AUTHOR

At just 19 years old, Lamla July brings a fresh perspective to the field of real estate and property management. With a passion for learning and an innate curiosity about the industry, I've dedicated countless hours to researching and studying the ins and outs of property management. Despite my young age, determination and commitment have allowed me to gain valuable insights into the field, making me well-equipped to share my knowledge with others.Lamla has a keen interest in real estate.Many investment, wealth-building, and personal-development opportunities are available in this sector.My enthusiasm for real estate at such a young age demonstrates my ambitions and forward-thinking mindset.Lamla is a real estate author who has written about a variety of topics in the business. I can delve into issues like market analysis, property management strategies, and legal considerations, among others. By imparting this real estate expertise and experiences, I have hopes to encourage others to research this lucrative industry and use it to their advantage.It is truly remarkable how committed Lamla has been to real estate at such a young age. It exhibits his ambition and willingness to take chances in order to achieve his objectives. He hopes to encourage other young people to follow their passions with confidence by sharing his experience as an author.I'm excited to present this thorough analysis of the subject at hand as a young and aspiring author. I'm a 19-year-old South African-born and raised boy with a strong interest in research and writing by the name of Lamla July. I've been studying this topic for a long time and have grown to have a strong passion for it, which has inspired me to explore the Real Estate.Good luck on your Real estate journey may God continue to bless you as you embark on your journey !!!

INDEX

R
- Real Estate Investment Trust (REIT)
- Real Estate Market Analysis
- Rental Property

S
- Seller's Market
- Short Sale
- Subprime Mortgage Crisis

T
- Title Insurance
- Transfer Tax

U
- Underwriting

V
- Vacancy Rate

W
- Zoning Laws